職人という生き方

The Way of Life as Craftsman

工匠的生活方式

駿河竹千筋細工

Suruga Bamboo Ware

駿河竹千筋細工

もくじ
Contents
目次
11

継承家業
家を継ぐ──
Taking over the family business

みやび行燈製作所
Miyabi Andon Factory
MIYABI 行燈製作所

自らの殻を破ることができた
大阪での接客修行時代
Got out of its shell during apprenticeship in concierge service in Osaka
突破自己的框梧
在大阪待客習藝的那段歲月

6年間の接客修行を乗り越え、
伝統工芸士の渡邊さんに弟子入り
Took apprenticeship to Tetsuo Watanabe, a Traditional Craftsman, after the one in concierge service for 6 years
待客居練歷時六載、
向傳統工藝士渡邊先生拜師學藝

駿河竹千筋細工の歴史 39
History of Suruga Bamboo Ware
駿河竹千筋細工的歷史

駿河竹千筋細工の魅力 45
Charm of Suruga Bamboo Ware
駿河竹千筋細工的魅力

「ひご」づくりは竹の性質を知ることから
Making "Higo" starts with learning characteristics of bamboo
「竹籤」的製作始於通曉竹子的特性

作品の善し悪しを左右する「曲げ」
Bending process that affects quality of products
左右作品好壞的「折彎」流程

駿河竹千筋細工のつくり方 49
How to Make Suruga Bamboo Ware
駿河竹千筋細工的製作方法

竹細工職人への道 55
Gateway to be a Bamboo Craftsman
成為竹藝工匠的路程

誰もが驚く駿河竹千筋細工をつくっていきたい
Passion for creation of Suruga Bamboo Ware to make everybody surprised
想做出讓人驚喜的駿河竹千筋細工

体験するなら・学ぶなら 62
To Experience & To Learn
體驗、學習

はじめに

Introduction 前言

地球の裏側の情報が瞬時に手に入り、他民族との接点も格段に増えた現代。私たちが、日本人であることを自らに問いかける機会が増えてきました。日本人の美意識を映し出す伝統工芸品に注目が集まるのも、そんな時代背景があるからと考えられます。確かにその土地に根ざした土、木、竹などの材料を用いて、日本人らしい創意工夫と四季のある国で育まれた感性、受け継いできた器用さをもって生み出される伝統工芸品には、日本人のアイデンティティがあると言えるかもしれません。

一方で伝統工芸品には、地場産業の中核を担ってきたという歴史があります。昨今の伝統工芸品産業の衰退は、地域経済に大きな打撃を与えています。時代の変化に翻弄され、代々続いてきた家業を次の代に引き継ぐことをためらう環境に置かれている伝統工芸従事者の多くは、自分の家族の生活はもちろん、日本人の期待や自分の街の将来という大きなものも同時に背負っているのです。「継ぐべき家がある」ということは、端から見ると時にうらやましくも見えますが、実は大変なことです。

これまでニッポンのワザドットコム編集部では、二代目、三代目となる後継者に対して多くの取材をしてきました。驚くことにそんなプレッシャーの中でも、後継者となる若者は時代の感覚を捉え、新しいマーケットを作り出すべく東奔西走しています。取材の後には、心に清涼な風が吹いたような清々しい気持ちになります。

本書は、もっと多くの方に彼らのことを知っていただきたいという思いでまとめたものです。彼らの手で、ふたたび日本人が誇りを取り戻し、日本らしさの中で日本経済が津々浦々から復興することを心から願っております。

Today, any kind of information from the other side of the world comes to hand in a blink, and opportunities to learn about different ethnic groups are drastically increasing. In this trend, there are more and more opportunities coming up to us Japanese to think about ourselves. Japanese traditional crafts reflecting our senses of beauty receive attention from people, and we think this has happened may be because of the mentioned background. It seems to be true that our traditional crafts, for which the craftsmen uses the local materials such as soil, wood, and bamboo, with senses of beauty developed in an effort of ingenuity in four different seasons and with artfulness inherited, represent the Japanese people's identify.

On the other hand, traditional crafts hold the own history that have taken a major role in development of the local industries. Declination of traditional craft industries delivers remarkable impact to local economies. Many of those working on traditional crafts, tossed about by changing times and in hesitation to hand their family business over to the next generation, take charges not only of their family's life but also of responding to expectations from people across the country and the future of their hometowns. To face the reality of "having family business to take over" is not as easy as it may sometimes look from outside.

We "nipponnowaza.com" have covered and taken many interviews with second and third generations of craftsmen. We have found surprisingly that those young generations are constantly on the move in order to capture today's sense and try to create new markets. After taking interviews with them we became refreshed as if the fresh wind blew into our minds.

We now would like to deliver this book to all the readers with our hope for better understanding of those young craftsmen by more people. We hope from the heart that they help us Japanese restore our pride and make the economies re-established all over the country while staying with Japanese touch.

Editorial Department of "nipponnowaza.com"
April 2012
http://www.nipponnowaza.com

在現在這個時代，我們可以瞬間取得地球另一端的資訊，接觸到其他民族機會也較以往增加了許多。我們日本人好好檢視自我的機會也增加了不少。傳統工藝品能反映出日本人的審美意識，因而會受到矚目也是由於其時代背景。的確，使用生長在這塊土地上的土壤、樹木、竹子等材料，加上日本人的創意與在這四季分明的國度自然形成的感性，配合與生俱來的巧手，這樣孕育出來的傳統工藝品裡，也許蘊藏著日本人的集體認同感吧。

另一方面，傳統工藝品過去曾經一直是地方產業的核心。近來，傳統工藝品產業的衰退，對地方經濟造成了很大的打擊。受到時代變化的翻弄，大多數的傳統工藝業者處於煩惱傳承世代家業的環境下，除了自己家人的生活，同時也背負著日本民族的期待和家鄉未來發展的重責大任。所謂「有必須傳承的家業」，從一旁看來好像很令人羨慕，其實真的是很辛苦的。

目前為止，日本的技藝.COM編輯部採訪了多位第二代、第三代的技藝繼任者。令人驚訝的是，即使在那樣的壓力中，身為繼任者的年輕人仍可以掌握著時代的脈動，努力為爭取新市場而東奔西走著。採訪後，感覺心裡好像吹過一陣涼風般地清爽。

本書是為了讓更多人知道他們的故事而編輯成冊的。希望他們的雙手，再次爭回日本人的榮耀，在日本式的風格中，衷心祈禱日本經濟能從全國各地復興重建。

2012年4月　日本的技藝.COM編輯部
http://www.nipponnowaza.com

2012年4月　ニッポンのワザドットコム編集部
http://www.nipponnowaza.com

家を継ぐ

継承家業

Taking over the family business

繊細な模様が印象的な駿河竹千筋細工の菓子器

A cake box of Suruga Bamboo Ware with its impressive patterns

駿河竹千筋細工的糕點器皿，式樣細緻令人印象深刻

自らの殻を破ることができた大阪での接客修行時代

　江戸の初期に始まった静岡の伝統工芸「駿河竹千筋細工」は、竹を細く裂いた「丸ひご」が醸し出す繊細さはもちろん、丈夫で長持ちし、徐々に飴色となる竹特有の経年変化も楽しめるのが魅力。鳥籠や菓子器を出品した明治6年（1873年）のウィーン国際博覧会では、各国から好評を博し、その後は日本を代表する輸出品として発展を遂げました。現在においては、伝統的な作品づくりから、趣向を凝らした作品まで幅広く制作されています。

　そんな伝統工芸の明日を担う三兄弟がいるとうかがい向かったのは、東海道新幹線「静岡」駅から車ですぐの住宅街に佇む「みやび行燈製作所」。出迎えてくれたのは、とても人懐っこい笑顔が印象的な三男・杉山茂靖さんでした。

　「高校生のときに、長男（現・社長）や次男（現・専務）とともに駿河竹千筋細工職人になり、家業を継ごうと決意しました。うちはすぐに修行をさせるのではなく、一度大阪の親戚が営む雛

駿河竹千筋細工職人の杉山茂靖さん（37歳）。杉山雅泰さん（駿河竹千筋細工職人、現・みやび行燈製作所会長）の三男として1974年に誕生。高校卒業後、6年間大阪の雛人形店で接客を学ぶ。2000年より、みやび行燈製作所にて、伝統工芸士・渡邊鉄夫さんに弟子入りし、数々の作品づくりに携わる

Shigeyasu Sugiyama, 37, a craftsman of Suruga Bamboo Ware. He was born as third son of Masayasu Sugiyama (A craftsman of Suruga Bamboo Ware and the Chairman of Miyabi Andon Factory today) in 1974. After graduating his high school he took apprenticeship to learn concierge service at a hina doll shop in Osaka for 6 years. In 2000, he then became apprenticeship to Tetsuo Watanabe, a Traditional Craftsman at Miyabi Andon Factory, and started to work on creating many products.

駿河竹千筋細工工匠，杉山茂靖先生（37歲）。他是杉山雅泰先生（駿河竹千筋細工工匠，現為MIYABI行燈製作所的董事長）的三男，生於1974年。高中畢業後，曾花6年在大阪的古裝玩偶店學習接客技巧。2000年開始在MIYABI行燈製作所，正式向傳統工藝士渡邊鐵夫先生拜師學藝，現在擁有許多作品。

「人形店で最低3年間接客を学ばせるのですが、私はそれまでとても引っ込み思案で人見知りの性格だったため、歩いてくる人全員に声をかけてお店に呼び込むなんてそれはもう苦痛で、逃げたくてしょうがなかったですね。でも、それが理由で静岡に帰るなんて言ったら、恥ずかしいし、大阪での修行を乗り越えた兄たちに合わせる顔がないと思いました。また、接客の仕事をしない限り、必要とされない人間となってしまうという危機感もどんどん膨らんでいったのです。それで、自分の殻を破り、まずは話し言葉を関西弁に変えることから始めました。決してうまいとは言えない関西弁でしたが、静岡訛りのある話し言葉より、お客さんの反応が良くなり、不思議と接客もうまくいったのです。また、上司がいつも温かく見守ってくれたことで、ホームシックで、折れそうになっていた心も何とか持ち堪えました。大阪は人情の街とも呼ばれていますが、見ず知らずの土地での一人暮らしでしたので、こうした優しさは一層心に染みましたね」。

6年間の接客修行を乗り越え、伝統工芸士の渡邊さんに弟子入り

6年にも及ぶ修行を乗り越え、晴れて兄弟とともに家業を継ぐことになって、約2年。杉山さんのお父様であり現会長が、伝統工芸士として活躍しながらも自らの工房をたたもうとしていた渡邊鉄夫さんに「今までに培ってきた技術を若手に伝えて欲しい」と、みやび行燈製作所への入社を依頼。このことをきっかけに、杉山さんは本格的な弟子入りを渡邊さんに志願したそうです。

「修行は小刀で竹を削ることから始まりました。そんなある日、削り続けていたら筋肉どころか骨にまで痛みが。渡邊さんにアドバイスを求めたところ『竹を削ろうと思うな』とだけ言われたのです。当時この言葉の意味が解らなかったのですが、今思うとこの言葉以上に適切な言葉はないと思いますね。つまり、削ろうと思うと小刀の刃が竹に深く入り、刃がスムーズに進まなくなるのですが、それをどうにかしようと力んでしまうので、"竹を削ろうと思うな"ということだったのです。この意味に気づいてから

駿河竹千筋細工職人の渡邊鉄夫さん（76歳）。16歳から修行をはじめ、27歳で独立。伝統的技術や技法の分析、そして後継者育成に貢献したことが評価され、42歳で駿河竹千筋細工の伝統工芸士に認定され、現在に至る

Tetsuo Watanabe, 76, a Traditional Craftsman of Suruga Bamboo Ware. He started his apprenticeship at the age of 16 and became independent at 27. For the great contribution he did on successor development, he was certified as a Traditional Craftsman at 42 and has kept its position up to today.

駿河竹千筋細工的工匠，渡邊鐵夫先生（76歲）。他從16歲開始修業習藝，27歲獨立創業。對傳統技術或技法的分析、以及新世代繼任者的培育貢獻良多，廣泛贏得高度評價，42歲獲得認定為駿河竹千筋細工的傳統工藝士，一直到現在。

は、肩の力も抜けて、小刀を扱える時間、そして削る竹の本数も飛躍的に伸びていきましたね」と修業時代を振り返る杉山さん。

また、渡邊さんは杉山さん以外の若手職人さんにも伝統の技術を教えていると言います。

「師匠は、毎週火曜日に私も参加している『若手育成会（技術保存会）』を開催しています。他の師匠に弟子入りしている若手の職人さんも参加しているのですが、普段指導を受けている師匠とは違う技術を学べるということで参加している職人さんも多いようです」と杉山さん。

右に左にと手で曲げるだけで、あっという間に
末端まで裂けていくその様子は、まるで手品のよう

The work, to make it split into strands only by bending
from side to side by hand, looks like a magic.

僅用手左右來回折彎，轉眼間就裂開到末端，看起來好像魔術一樣。

「胴乱（どうらん）」を熱し、竹を丸くします。
この道具は、戦前から使われているものだそうです

裂いた竹を、刃のついた小さな穴へと
順番に通せば、「ひご」の完成です。
鮮やかな手つきに、思わず見とれます

"Higos" become complete by getting the strands
of bamboo in sequence into a small hole where
a blade is formed. You may become absorbed in
the scene of the smooth work.

將裂開的竹條依序穿過附有刀刃的孔洞，這樣
即完成「竹籤」製作。俐落的手法讓人不禁看
得著迷。

A tool called Doran, heated
when making bamboo materials
into rounded shape. This tool
has been said in use since before
the War.

將「胴亂」加熱用以折彎竹條。
聽說這項工具從戰前用到現在。

20

筒状のマイクカバーの制作依頼を受けた際につくった直径4センチの「丸曲げ」(写真中央)。「今までに制作したことのない小ささでしたので、コテで曲げてから、鉋と鑿で丸曲げの接合部分をつくりました。完成するまで苦労しましたよ」と渡邊さん

A circular piece "Maru-mage (bent in rounded shape)" of 40mm in diameter made upon a specific order for a tubular microphone cover (center in photo). "This was in the smallest size I have never experienced so I had to create specific area on it by using a plane and a chisel for circular connection. It was a tough work", says Mr. Watanabe.

之前客戶要求製作圓筒狀的麥克風蓋子時,特別製作出來的直徑4公分的「圓環」(照片中央)。渡邊先生說:「目前為止沒有製作過這麼小尺寸的,因此以棒狀工具折彎後使用鉋刀和鑿刀製作出彎曲的接合部分。這項任務真是辛苦啊!」

1.「『四角曲げ』では、竹を一気に曲げるのでなく、竹が割れないように、曲げるところの周辺を熱してから曲げるのがポイントです」と渡邊さん
2. 四角曲げをした竹は、鉋と鑿などで、接合部分に隙間ができないように調節し、接着剤で固めます

1. "For 'Shikaku-mage (bent in rectangular shape)', in order not to make the material broken, the point you must keep in mind is to heat the area around the portion prior to bending, never try to bend it at once", says Mr. Watanabe.
2. After "Shikaku-mage" completed, the craftsman finishes the connection area by plane and chisel in order not to leave gap, and make it connected by adhesive.

1. 渡邊先生說:「在進行『四角彎曲』時,不能一次就將竹子折彎,重點是要小心在折彎處加熱以免竹子斷裂。」
2. 四角彎曲後的竹條,用鉋刀和鑿刀等將接合部分調整到沒有縫隙,再用黏膠固定。

「ひご」づくりは竹の性質を知ることから

2階に工房があるということで、実際の仕事風景を見学させていただくことにしました。

「駿河竹千筋細工の繊細さの象徴でもある『丸ひご』。そのつくり方を紹介します。まずは、竹の寸法を測り、ノコギリで切ってから、煮込むことで油を抜いて強度を増強。これを、乾かしすぎて弾力がなくならないよう注意しながら数ヶ月間乾燥させます。竹といっても真竹や孟宗竹などいくつもの種類があるので、それぞれの特長に配慮する必要もありますね。次に、竹の皮を削り、竹の繊維を壊さないように裂け目を入れ、右に左にと手で曲げて末端まで裂きます。最後に、『竹ひご引き』（鉄板に刃のある大小様々な穴を開けた道具）で、荒引き、中引き、仕上げ引きと順番に細い穴へと通していけば、角のとれた細い『丸ひご』の出来上がりとなります」。

作品の善し悪しを左右する「曲げ」

次に杉山さんに紹介していただいたのは、駿河竹千筋細工づくりの工程において最も難しく、作品の善し悪しを左右する「曲げ」。

「夏場の『曲げ』は、熱して冷めるまでの間に竹が伸びます。逆に、冬場は縮むので、竹の伸縮も考慮しながら制作しなければなりません。『胴乱』という道具を熱して、竹ひごを曲げる『丸曲げ』が基本としてありますが、師匠はコテを熱して曲げる高度な技術『四角曲げ』も得意としています。単純に考えても、4回の曲げの中での歪みと、伸縮によるすべての歪みを計算しなくてはならないわけです。最後に、「曲げ」工程以前につけておいた目印を見ながら、キリなどで穴を開けます。そこに「ひご」を通せば、作品の完成。『四角曲げ』などの高度な技術を学べること、そして何より師匠に出会えたことに感謝しています」と杉山さんは笑顔で語ります。

渡邊さんが復活させた伝統模様「あわじ結び」。
「作品を手にとり、軽さや丈夫さを感じて欲しい」と杉山さん

A traditional pattern "Awaji-musubi" that Mr. Watanabe revived.
"I hope people take up my product and feel its lightness and robustness",
says Mr. Sugiyama.

渡邊先生製作出的傳統式樣「吉祥結」。
杉山先生說:「希望客人拿著我們的作品時能感受到輕巧和堅實。」

誰もが驚く駿河竹千筋細工を
つくっていきたい

最後に、杉山さんが職人として目指すところをうかがいました。

「祖父の時代には約80名の職人さんがいたと聞いていますが、現在は約13名しかいなくなりました。昔はつくれば売れた時代でしたが、今は違う。ライフスタイルが和から洋へと移り変わったように、時代のニーズに合った駿河竹千筋細工が求められているのです。伝統的なものづくりも大事ですが、残ってこそ、伝統工芸だと思っていますので、伝統の技術と新しい感覚を融合させた誰もが驚く今までにない駿河竹千筋細工を、兄弟みんなでつくっていきたいと考えています。また、その中でどんな依頼にも応えていこうと考えています。それは、断らない姿勢こそ職人にとって大切ですし、様々な経験を積むことで作品づくりに幅が生まれると実感しているためです。今では、こうした姿勢に共感してくれる方々も増え、新しい仕事に挑戦できることも多くなりました」。

「安く、誰もが手の届くものを」ではなく、「高くとも、手に入れることでステータスとなる逸品を」。その思いのもと、数々の伝統工芸に課せられた〝生き残り〟という使命にも似た問題に立ち向かう、杉山さんを始めとする、みやび行燈製作所の皆さん。その情熱あふれる姿に、本物とは何か、伝統とは何かということを深く考えさせられました。

郷土工芸品「駿河和染め」を用いたバッグは、
ジーンズなどのカジュアルな服装にも似合いそう

Bags with a local craftwork "Suruga Wazome (dying)"
incorporated look nice with casual dress, even such as jeans.

用於鄉土藝品「駿河和染」的竹籃，好像也適合搭配牛仔褲等輕鬆的服裝。

Got out of its shell during apprenticeship in concierge service in Osaka

A Shizuoka's local art craft "Suruga Bamboo Ware", which dates back to the early Edo period, is featured not only with its preciseness realized by Maruhigo made with strands of bamboo but also with its robustness for long life and the color tone that changes to light brown as time goes because of bamboo's particularity. At the International Expo held in Vienna in Meiji 6 (1873) where craftsmen placed their bird cages and cake boxes on show, the arts attracted visitors from many countries, and then it has become developed as one of Japan's representative exporting products. Today, a wide variety of products from traditional ones to those with elaborate decorative works are produced. The factory we visited was Miyabi Andon Factory, placed in a residential distinct in a short drive from Shizuoka station of Shinkansen, that we were told three brothers are striving to lead tomorrow's traditional art crafts. The person welcomed us was the 3rd-oldest brother Shigeyasu Sugiyama, with an impressive friendly smile.

"When I was a high school student, I made up my mind to become a craftsman and to take over the family business together with my oldest brother (current President) and his second-oldest brother (current Managing Director). To respect our family's policy I started my ascetic training by learning concierge service for 3 years at a doll shop that our relatives operates in Osaka, not started apprenticeship on bamboo craft directly. As I was very shy and reserved with strangers at that time, the work of calling everybody walking on the street was really a tough for me therefore I wanted to get out of it. But I thought I could not say I wanted to go back to home only with this kind of reason, and thought I might be unable to face my brothers who had got over their training in the same way in Osaka if I would do so. At the same time, a sense of crisis had been developed in my mind that myself would become a needless person unless being able to serve customers. Therefore I started to get out of my shell and to switch my spoken language to Osaka dialect. My Osaka dialect had never become perfect, but compared to my original spoken language with Shizuoka accent it worked well to win customer's attention and my concierge service started working better strangely. Also as my boss kept him warmly watched over me all the time I could marginally survive. Osaka is called a town of human empathy, and as I was living alone there, gentleness of people really touched my heart."

Took apprenticeship to Tetsuo Watanabe, a Traditional Craftsman, after the one in concierge service for 6 years

It has been about 2 years since he took over his family business after he finished his apprenticeship for as long as 6 years. The Chairman, who is his father, asked Tetsuo Watanabe, who had kept working as a Traditional Craftsman but was going to close his factory, to employ him at Miyabi Andon Factory to hand techniques over to the next young generation. This triggered Mr. Sugiyama to apply for full apprenticeship to Mr. Watanabe.

"My apprenticeship started by shaving bamboo material with a knife. On day when I kept the shaving work I felt pain not only in a muscle but also in bone. I asked Mr. Watanabe for advice and he only said 'Do not try to shave the bamboo'. I could not understand what he meant at that time, but I now feel there is no more suggestive message than it. The more I try shave, the more the knife bites into the material and it does not smoothly go forward. Then I put more force unconsciously to manage this situation… I finally understood why he said 'Do not try to shave the bamboo'. After that, I could become able to relax my shoulders, keep knifing work longer, and the number of bamboo materials I work on per day jumped up", Mr. Sugiyama looks back on his apprenticeship period.

Mr. Sugiyama also says Mr. Watanabe teaches his techniques not only to him.

"My superior holds an event 'Young players development school (Tradition preservation school)' on every Tuesday that I participate in. Young craftsmen who work under other superiors participate in this, and the benefit for many of them is to have opportunities to learn techniques that are different from those learned from their superiors", says Mr. Sugiyama.

突破自己的桎梏在大阪待客習藝的那段歲月

靜岡的傳統工藝「駿河竹千筋細工」始於江戶初期，其使用細圓「竹籤」編製營造出的不只細緻，還有經久耐用的特質，竹子在多年後會隨著時間的變遷而變成琥珀色，這就是竹子的魅力。明治6年（1873年），在維也納國際博覽會上展出的鳥籠和糕點器皿博得了各國的高度評價，此後，該項工藝成為代表日本的出口貨品而獲得了良好的發展。目前，從傳統的工藝品製作，到別出心裁的作品，創作範圍十分廣泛。肩負著這項傳統工藝的未來的是一家三兄弟，前往拜訪位於住宅區裡的「MIYABI行燈製作所」，從東海道新幹線「靜岡」站搭車不久即可到達。前來迎接的人是老三杉山茂靖，他總是帶著令人印象深刻的開朗笑容。

「高中的時候，大兒子（現任總經理）和二兒子（常務董事）都決定要繼承家業，成了駿河竹千筋細工的工匠。家裡並沒有立即讓我學習技藝，而是叫我去大阪親戚經營的古裝玩偶店至少學習三年的待客技巧，我在那時候以前非常畏縮不前，因為怕生的個性，對登門的所有客人打招呼，請客人進來參觀之類的，真的感到很痛苦，非常想逃離。但是，如果以這個理由回靜岡的話，我會感到很慚愧，沒臉見過通過了大阪學習修練的哥哥們。而且，不做接待客人的工作就會變成沒有貢獻的人，這樣的危機意識日漸增加。之後，要突破我自己的桎梏，我決定先把口語變成關西方言。雖然不能說是絕對流暢的關西方言，但比起帶有靜岡腔調的口語，客人的反應變好了，神奇的是待客技巧也變得更熟練了。而且，上司一直都對我寄與厚望，因為想念家鄉，曾經感到快要屈服的心情也總算堅持了下來。雖說大阪也被認為是個很有人情味的城市，但在人生地不熟的地方一個人生活，這樣的親切感就更深入人心啊。」

待客磨練歷時六載，向傳統工藝士渡邊先生拜師學藝

結束了長達六年的修業習藝生活，風光地和兄弟們一起繼承家業約2年時間。杉山先生的父親，即現任董事長對渡邊鐵夫這位頗有名望卻想關閉自己工房的傳統工藝士說：「希望您能把至今所學的技藝傳授給年輕人」，於是聘請他到MIYABI行燈製作所工作。據說正是藉此機緣，杉山先生才正式向渡邊師傅提出了拜師學藝的請求。

回想起當年，杉山說「修業習藝要從用小刀削竹子開始。有一天，削著削著，那種疼痛不光是肌肉甚至滲透到了骨子裡了。於是，我便向渡邊師傅求教，沒料到師傅只說了一句：「不要想成是在削竹子」。當時我並不了解這句話的涵義，現在回想起來真的是沒有比這句話更合適的了。也就是說，一想到削的話，小刀的刀刃就會深入竹子，這樣一來刀刃就不會順利地向前，想著總得想個辦法的時候，就會不由得更用力，因此師傅才會說：「不要想成是在削竹子」。當我意識到這個涵義後，肩部就放輕鬆了，操作小刀的時間、以及所削竹子的數量也得到了飛快的成長。」

還有，除了杉山先生，渡邊先生也將傳統技藝傳授給了其他年輕工匠。

杉山先生說：「師傅會在每周二召開『新人培訓會（技術保存會）』，我也有參加。其他師傅的年輕門徒也會來參加，因為學到的技巧與平時的師傅不同，所以來參加的工匠很多。」

Lighting equipment "SEN" created in collaboration with Toshiyuki Tani, a lighting creator. "We did not have right understanding on requirements specified in his drawings, and he, the lighting creator, did not have knowledge in detail on our Suruga Bamboo Ware. Thus we asked him to stay in Shizuoka for several nights to share a comprehensive image of the product we had to jointly finish", says Mr. Sugiyama.

與照明作家谷俊幸先生共同合作的照明「SEN」。杉山先生說:「我們不了解設計圖上細微的設計,而作家他也不甚了解駿河竹千筋細工。因此,直到完成為止,要請作家在靜岡住宿幾晚,以便雙方能了解彼此的概念。」

照明作家の谷俊幸氏とコラボレーションして作り上げた照明「SEN」。「私たちは設計図上の細かなデザインが理解できなかったし、作家さんは駿河竹千筋細工のことを詳しく知らなかった。ですので、完成するまで作家さんに静岡に何泊かしてもらい完成イメージを共有することで出来上がりました」と杉山さん

Making "Higo" starts with learning characteristics of bamboo

We were allowed to step into his atelier located at the second floor.

"I would like to introduce you how to make 'Maru-higo' that represents the preciseness of Suruga Bamboo Ware. First to do is to measure the size of material, cut it into pieces by a saw, and to boil it to deoil and develop strength. We then leave it for drying, for several months, not too much in order to maintain certain elasticity. As there are many different types of bamboos such as Madake and Mosochiku, you have to take each of the characteristics into consideration. Then strip the skin, make slits while not breaking the strings, and get them into strands by bending it from side to side. At the last step, get the strands go through 'Takehigo-hiki' (a tool with holes of various sizes with blades), from smaller to larger holes, to obtain thin Maru-higo with rounded sectional shape."

Bending process that affects quality of product

The next process Mr. Sugiyama introduced us was "Mage (bending)", the most difficult one in Suruga Bamboo Ware making process and be the key driver for quality of product.

"If you perform Mage by heating in summer, the length of bamboo material becomes longer until it gets cool. In contrast, it gets shorter in winder, so you have to consider such expansion and contraction when you perform it. The basics is 'Maru-mage', using a tool called Doran heated to bend bamboo strands, and my superior is also good at performing a higher technique called 'Shikaku-mage' using a heated iron for bending. Maru-mage is performed only at once, but Shikaku-mage is performed in four steps. If you think it simply, you should be able to imagine that you must take into consideration all the strains possibly happen while bending performed four times and the related expansion and contraction. Lastly you make holes by a wimble with the help of symbols marked prior to performing Mage process. Final products become complete after getting Higos go through the holes. I feel grateful for opportunities to learn high techniques such as Shikaku-mage, and more than that, I met my superior", Mr. Sugiyama explains with a smile.

Passion for creation of Suruga Bamboo Ware to make everybody surprised

Lastly, Mr. Sugiyama talked to us about the way he wants to go as a craftsman.

"I heard there used to be about 80 craftsmen working here when my grandfather was operating this factory, but now we only have 13. The more we produced the more sold in the past, but that is no longer the case. Like our lifestyle changed from Japanese to Western, we have to adapt Suruga Bamboo Ware to the needs of the time. Respecting traditional way of product making is important, and another important thing is to have our art craft survived, so I want to make unprecedented Suruga Bamboo Ware by merging traditional techniques and new sense, in collaboration with all my brothers. In this effort, I also would like try to respond to any kind of order. It is because I believe the attitude of saying yes is important for craftsmen to maintain and experiencing a wide variety of activities further develops my way of product making. Today, there are more and more people empathic to this way of thinking, and opportunities to challenge new things are increasing."

Not "Commodities for everyone at a low price" but "Valuable products for those who feel pleasure to own them even at a high price". With such mind, Mr. Sugiyama and the craftsmen of Miyabi Andon Factory are striving hard for "survival", a common challenge like a mission that a variety of traditional art crafts faces. Their passionate attitude made us think of what the real thing is, what the tradition means.

「竹籤」的製作始於通曉竹子的特性
因為工房就在二樓，所以就近參觀了實際的製作情景。
『細圓竹籤』象徵著駿河竹千筋細工的細緻。我來介紹一下製作方法吧。首先要測量竹子的尺寸，用鋸子鋸了之後煮透，接著去除油脂以增加強度。然後乾燥幾個月，同時要注意避免竹子過乾而失去彈性。竹子有真竹、孟宗竹等多個品種，所以也要顧慮到各種竹子的特性。接著，削什皮，先弄出裂縫同時要避免破壞到竹子的纖維，然後用手左右折彎讓竹子裂開到末端。最後，用『竹籤拉板』（鐵板上帶有大小孔的工具），按照粗拉、細拉、精拉的順序拉伸，只要依次穿過更細的孔，沒有稜角的『細圓竹籤』就可大功告成。」

左右作品好壞的「折彎」流程
接下來杉山先生介紹的是，駿河竹千筋細工製作過程中最難的「折彎」，這項流程能左右作品的好壞。
杉山笑著說：「夏天在『折彎』流程時，加熱到冷卻之間，竹子會增長。相反的，冬天時會收縮，所以製作同時要考慮到竹子的伸縮特性。把『胴亂』這個工具加熱後，用於將竹籤『折圓』是最基本的製作方法，老工匠也擅長把棒狀工具加熱後進行『四角折彎』，那是種高度技術。圓形折一次，四角要折四次。即使單純地想，四次折彎時會產生扭曲，還有竹子本身的伸縮也會造成的扭曲，故必須精密計算。最後，對照折彎前做好的記號進行鑿孔。接著，穿入「竹籤」後這個作品就算完成了。非常幸運地能學到『四角折彎』的技巧，總之非常感謝老師傅的教導。」

想做出讓人驚喜的駿河竹千筋細工
最後，杉山先生談到了身為工匠的理念。
「聽說祖父那個年代約有80位工匠，但是現在減少到了只有13人左右。以前只要做好就賣得出去，但現在時代不一樣了。如同生活方式從和式慢慢改變為西式一樣，駿河竹千筋細工要能順應時代的需求而改變。傳統的物品製作也很重要，正因為傳承至今才叫做傳統工藝，所以想要兄弟們一起做出前所未有的、融合了傳統技術和全新特色的駿河竹千筋細工。並且，其中還要能夠對應客戶的各種要求。這樣積極的態度對工匠來說真的非常重要，因為能夠透過累積各種經驗導引出自己的潛能。現在，擁有相同理念的朋友也在增加，可以挑戰的新工作也愈來愈多。」
以杉山先生為代表的MIYABI行燈製作所的工匠都認為，想創作的並不是「便宜、誰都買得起工藝品」，而是「高貴、但買到就能彰顯品位的傑作」。基於此想法，肩負著類似於各種傳統工藝中「傳承」的使命。他們以充滿熱情的態度促使我們深深思考何謂真品、何謂傳統。

連絡先／有限会社みやび行燈製作所　住所／静岡県静岡市葵区四番町 11-8
電話／ 054-252-2581　營業時間／ 9:00 〜 18:00
HP ／ http://miyabiandon.shop-pro.jp/

Contact: Miyabi Andon Factory Ltd. Address: 11-8, 4-bancho, Aoi-ku, Shizuoka City, Shizuoka
Phone: 054-252-2581 Opening hours: 9:00–18:00
Website: http://miyabiandon.shop-pro.jp/

聯絡處／有限会社 MIYABI 行燈製作所　地址／靜岡縣靜岡市葵區四番町 11-8
電話／ 054-252-2581　營業時間／ 9:00 〜 18:00
HP ／ http://miyabiandon.shop-pro.jp/

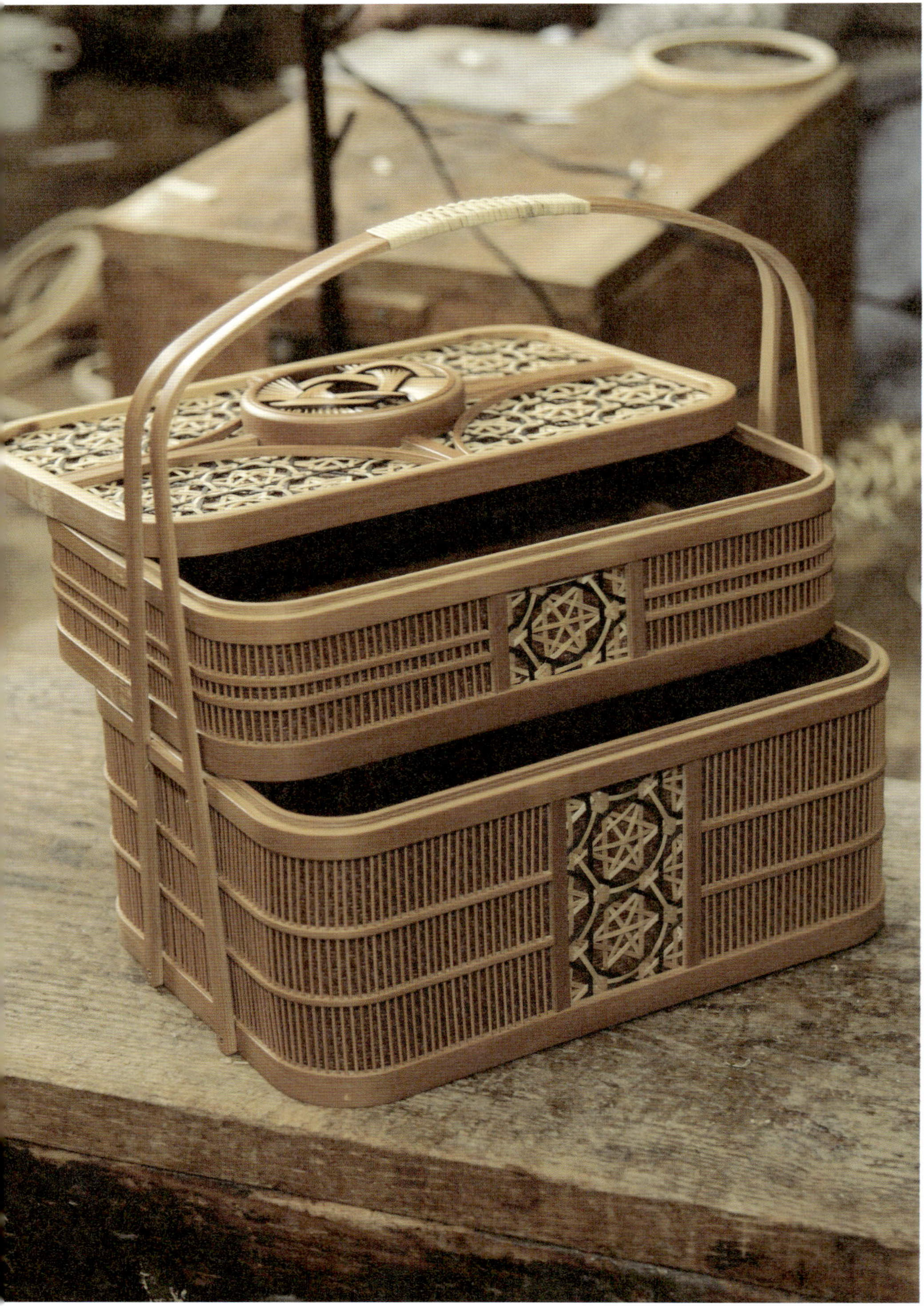

みやび行燈製作所　作
By Miyabi Andon Factory
MIYABI 行燈製作所 製作

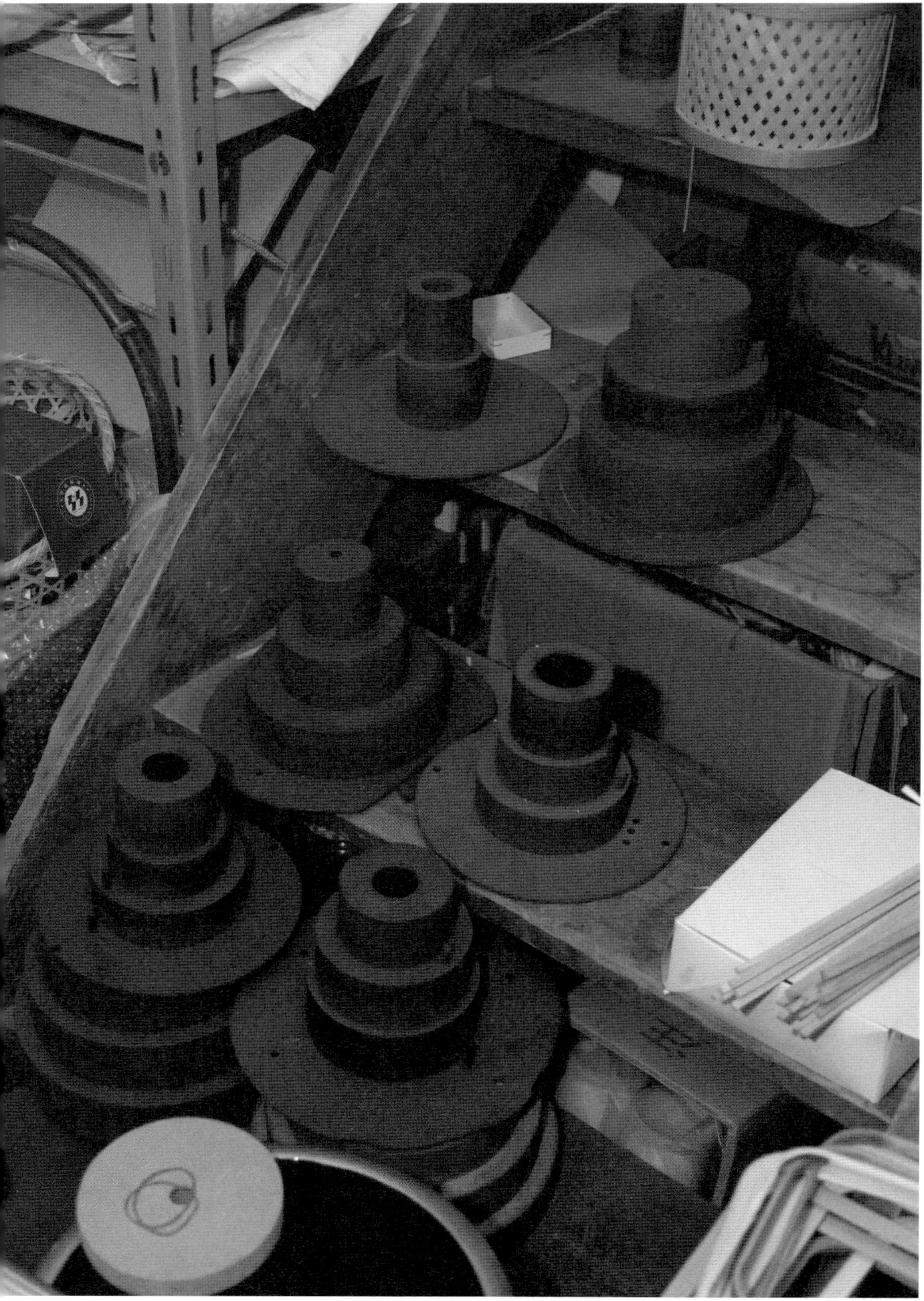

駿河竹千筋細工の歴史

History of Suruga Bamboo Ware

駿河竹千筋細工的歷史

徳川家康の鷹狩りの餌箱から
始まったともいわれる千筋細工

弥生時代の遺跡「登呂遺跡」から、竹製のザルも発見されている静岡の地で、駿河竹千筋細工が始まったのは江戸時代初期のこと。徳川家康が、駿府城に大御所として隠居していた際に、鷹狩りの餌箱を竹ひごでつくらせたのが始まりという説もあります。

その後の天保11年（1840年）頃、三河国（現在の愛知県東部）の岡崎藩士「菅沼一我」が静岡に立ち寄った際、宿泊した「はなや」の息子「清水猪兵衛」に、竹細工の技法を伝えました。以降、清水猪兵衛は弟子を育てる一方で、自らも今までにないほど繊細な虫籠や菓子器をつくり、広めて行きました。明治6年（1873年）にはウィーン国際博覧会にて日本の特産品として出品され、好評を博しました。それ以来、日本を代表する輸出品として、海外からの脚光を浴び、今日まで発展を続けています。

歌川国貞　辰巳芸妓図　江戸期（1828年頃）　協力／羽黒洞

Utagawa Kunisada, Tatsumigeiko-zu Edo Period (in around 1828) Courtesy: Hagurodo

歌川国贞　辰己芸妓图　江戸時代文化時期　協賛／羽黒洞

The origin of bamboo sensuji crafts, said to be a bait cage made Ieyasu Tokugawa ordered for falconry

The origination of Suruga Bamboo Ware dates back to the early Edo period in Shizuoka, which holds Toro Ruin of Yayoi period where bamboo baskets were discovered. The origin is said to be a bait cage made with bamboo higos for the use of falconry that Ieyasu Tokugawa ordered after he retired and living at Suruga Castle as the great old man. Later, in Tempo 11 (1840) or around, when Ichiga Suganuma, the feudal lord of Okazaki, Mikawanokuni (east part of Aichi today) stopped over Shizuoka, he stayed at Hanaya and taught the son Ihe-e Shimizu the bamboo craft techniques. Ihe-e Shimizu then created his products like insect cages and cake boxes in more precise style than ever and promoted the name, while nurturing his apprentices. In Meiji 6 (1873), Suruga Bamboo Ware was placed on the show as a Japan's special local product at the International Expo held in Vienna, and this attracted great interests. Since then Suruga Bamboo Ware has kept its position as one of Japan's representative exporting products and gathered much attention from overseas.

也有人說千筋細工是始於德川家康裝獵鷹誘餌的籃子

駿河竹千筋細工可追溯自江戶時代初期，在今天的靜岡有個彌生時代的「登呂遺址」，當地還發現了竹篩。據說源於德川家康隱居在駿府城時，也有一說，其始於德川家康裝獵鷹誘餌的籃子是用竹籤製作而成的。之後在天保11年（1840）左右，三河國（位於現在的愛知縣東部）的岡崎藩士「菅沼一我」在路經靜岡時，把竹製工藝傳授給投宿旅舍「HANAYA」的兒子「清水豬兵衛」。從此，清水豬兵衛一邊培養學徒，一邊自己編製當時還沒有的精緻蟲籠、糕點器皿。明治6年（1873年）時，作為日本的特產在維也納國際博覽會展出，贏得了相當高度的評價。從此，作為日本的代表性出口品，在海外逐漸顯露頭角而得以發展至今。

協力／羽黒洞　住所／東京都文京区湯島 4-6-11　湯島ハイタウン
電話／03-3815-0431　営業時間／11:00 〜 6:30　定休日／日曜休廊
HP ／ http:// www.hagurodo.jp

Courtesy: Hagurodo,　Address: Yushima Hightown, 4-6-11 Yushima, Bunkyo-ku, Tokyo
Telephone: 03-3805-0431,　Opening hours: 11:00 – 18:30,　Closed: Sundays
Website: http:// www.hagurodo.jp

協賛／羽黒洞　地址／東京都文京區湯島 4-6-11 湯島 High Town
電話／03-3815-0431　營業時間／11:00 〜 18:30　公休日／週日
網址／http:// www.hagurodo.jp

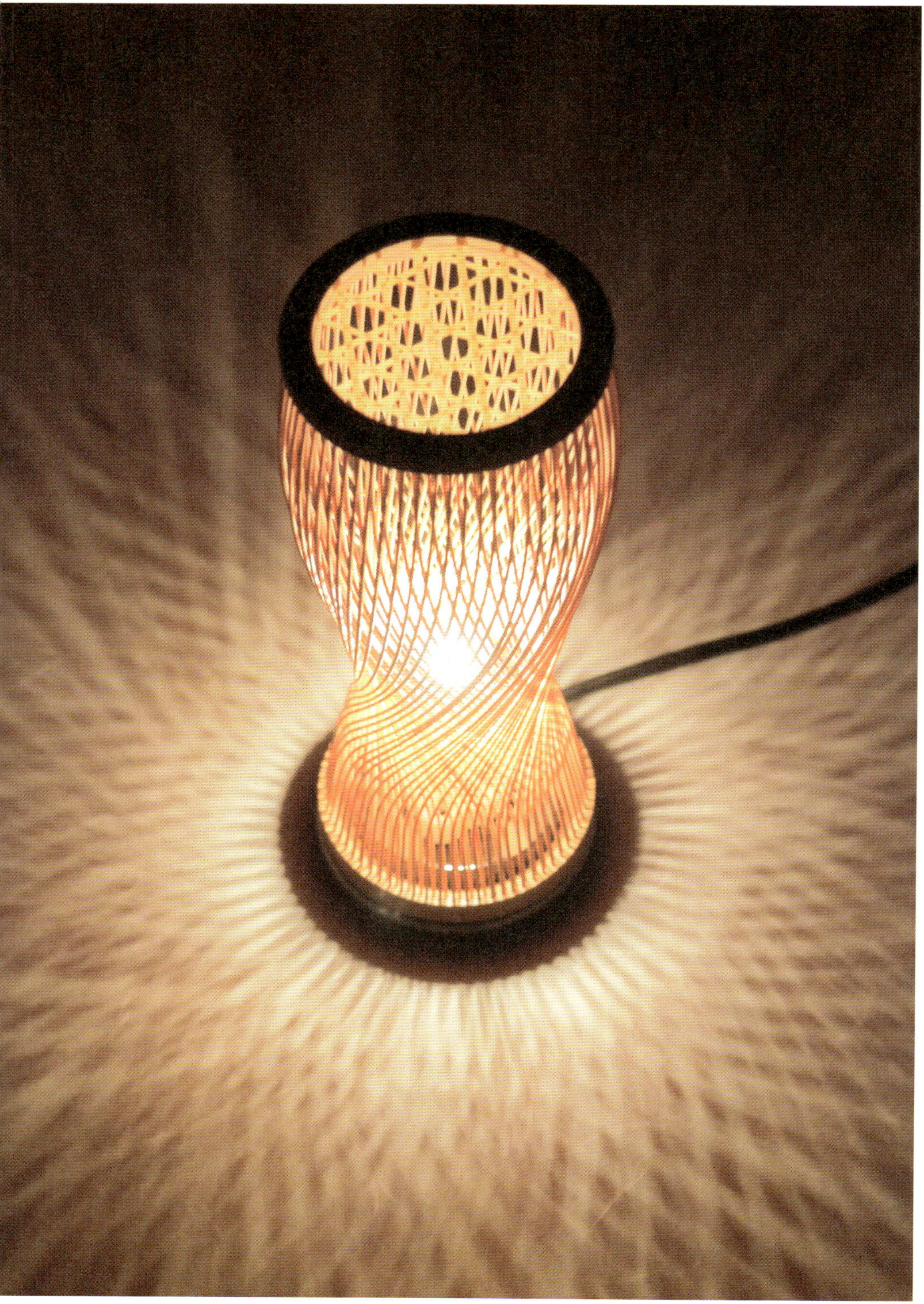

駿河竹千筋細工の魅力

Charm of Suruga Bamboo Ware

駿河竹千筋細工的魅力

現代的な家にも合うインテリア性。
時と共に風格ある色合いに変化

駿河竹千筋細工は、他の産地と違い「千筋ひご」と呼ばれる、細く丸く削った竹ひごをしなやかに曲げ、竹の輪に組み込んでゆくのが特長。完成した品を手にすると、丸ひごの持つあたたかく柔らかい肌ざわりを感じることができます。また、花器・菓子器・手提げ・虫籠・灯り・屏風・しおりなどといった生活に根ざした品から、風鈴などの季節を楽しむ品まで豊富に揃い、そのどれもが高いインテリア性を持つため、現代的な住居にもマッチ。使うほどに侘び・寂びの漂う、竹特有の風格ある経年変化も一つの楽しみといえます。

Nicely fits interiors of modern houses, the color increases its moral tone across the ages

Differently from those from other regions, Suruga Bamboo Ware is produced by bending Sensuji Higos, thousands of thin strands of bamboo with rounded sectional shape, and by having them assembled into a bamboo ring. Once you take the product, you will feel warm and soft texture of the Maru-higos. A wide range of products are offered, from those we are familiar with in our life such as flower pots, cake boxes, handbags, insect cages, lamps, folding screens, bookmarkers, to specialties we can enjoy sensing different seasons such as wind bells. All of those nicely fit interiors of modern houses. Another delight you can enjoy is that the color becomes aged with moral tone as it goes through time.

合於現代家居的室內裝飾別具風格的色調隨時代而變化

駿河竹千筋細工有別於其他產地的工藝品，使用又細又圓且極富彈性的「千筋竹籤」，能夠自然折彎編製竹環，此乃一大特色。將完成品拿在手中，可以感受到竹籤溫潤柔軟的觸感。從花器、糕點器皿、手提籃、蟲籠、燈具、屏風、書籤等一般生活用品，到風鈴等具有季節風情的製品，種類極為豐富。因為每一項製品都相當適於室內裝飾，因此也能搭配現代家居。竹子經年累月會散發出的閒寂古樸的特有韻味，那也可說是使用時的一大樂趣。

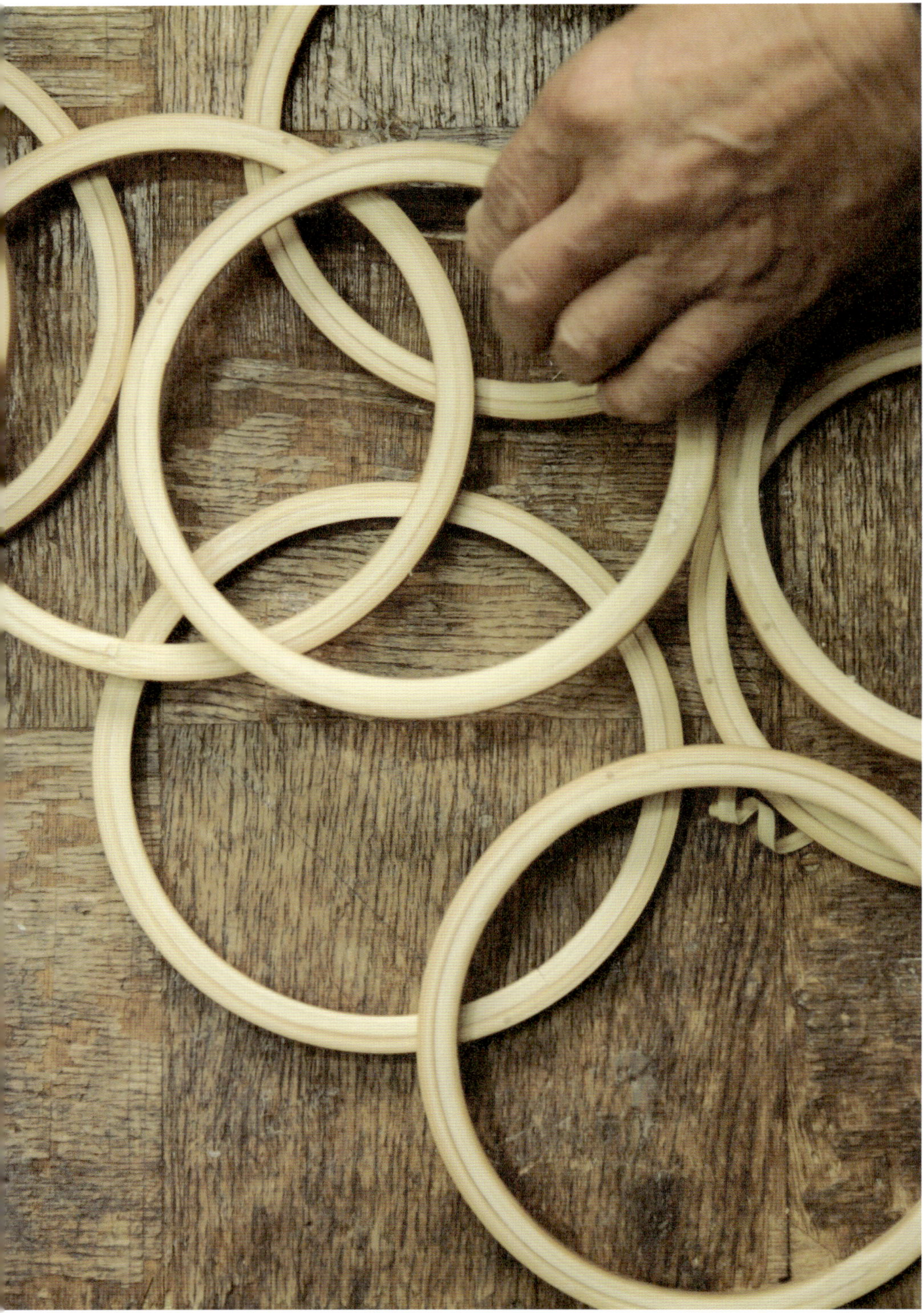

駿河竹千筋細工のつくり方

How to Make Suruga Bamboo Ware

駿河竹千筋細工的製作方法

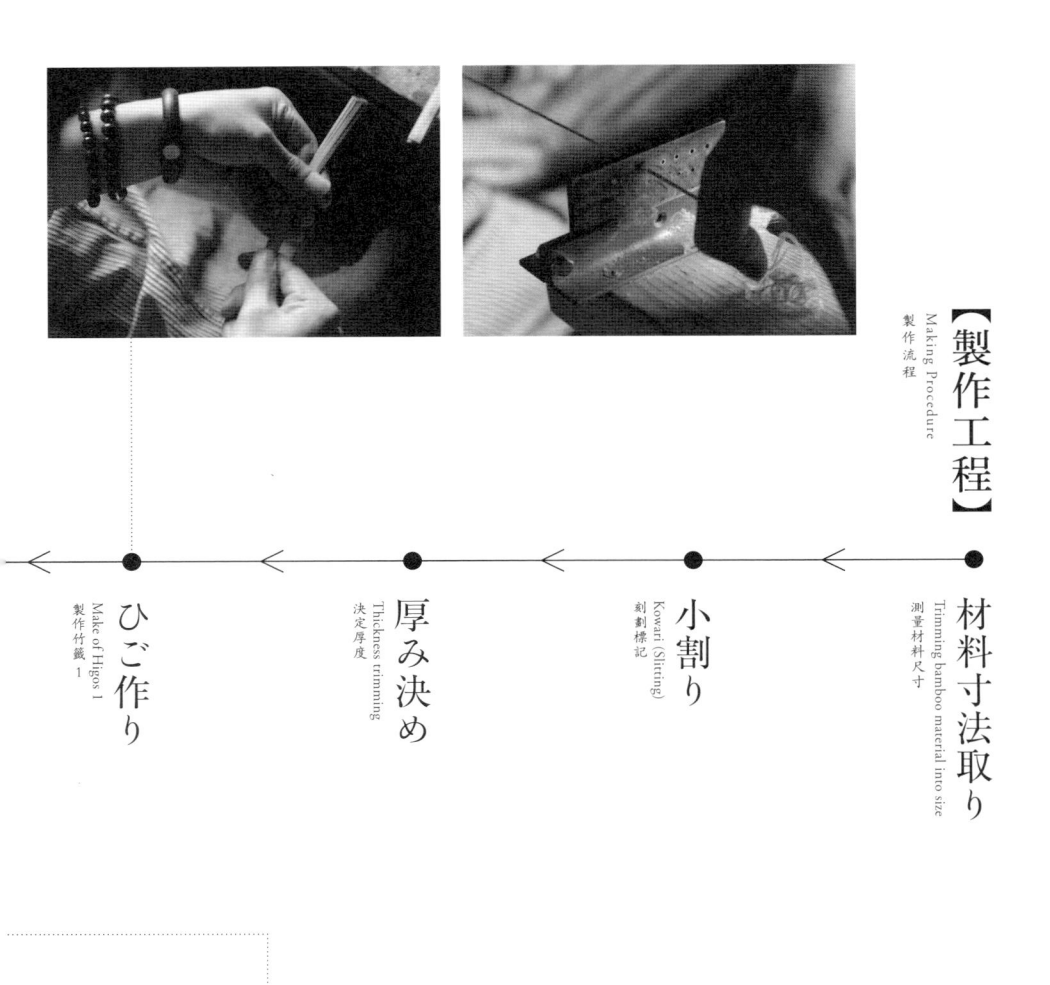

【製作工程】
Making Procedure
製作流程

← ひご作り
Make of Higos 1
製作竹籤1

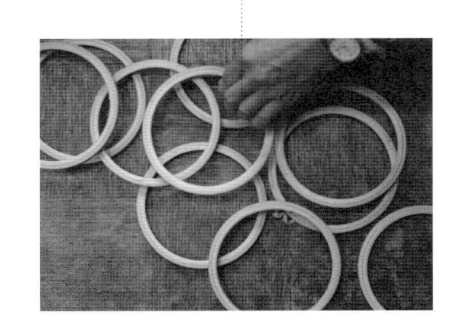

← 厚み決め
Thickness trimming
決定厚度

← 小割り
Kowari (Slitting)
刻割標記

← 材料寸法取り
Trimming bamboo material into size
測量材料尺寸

完成品 ← 組み立て ← 穴あけ ← 曲げ ← 輪作り

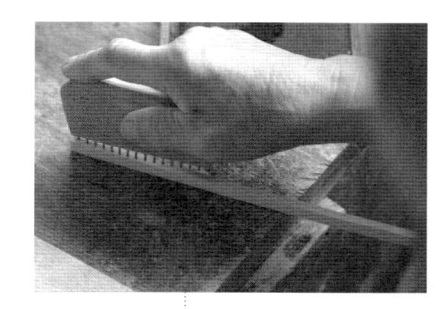

完成品 Finished product 完成品

組み立て Assembling 穿插組合

穴あけ Make of holes 鑽孔

曲げ Mage (Bending) 折彎

輪作り Make of rings 製作竹環

丸い竹ひごを本体にさし、継手という独特の技法で組む

駿河竹千筋細工の特徴は細く丸い竹ひご作りにあります。まずは、このひごを作ります。ものさしで寸法をはかりながら鋸（のこぎり）で竹を切り、竹の皮を削ったのち、なたで必要な寸法に割っていきます。

つぎに「せん台」という道具で厚みを決め、二本の刃をたてて細かい切り込みをいれる「小割り」で、細かい切込みを入れた後、手で左右に曲げながら竹を裂きます。裂いた竹をさらに、鉄板の穴に通して丸い竹ひごを作ります。穴は、太い物から細い物まであり、荒引き、中引き、仕上げ引きというように段々と細い穴に通すことで、きれいな丸ひごに仕上げていきます。ひごを通す枠も竹で作ります。ひご作りと同様にせん台で厚みを決めた後、ひごを通す場所に印を付けておきます。

印をつけた竹を熱して、輪や四角に曲げて冷まします。曲げた後を斜めに切って接着。この継ぎ手がわからないようにするのも腕の見せ所。輪や四角の枠の印のところに穴を開け、竹ひごを通

52

Putting Maru-higos into a body, and make them assembled by a unique method called Tsugite

Higos in rounded and thin shape take the major position of the specialties of Suruga Bamboo Ware. First to do is to make the higos. Cut bamboo material into pieces by measuring the length with a scale, peel the skin, and make it split in required width using Naga (a chopper). Trim the thickness by using a tool called Sendai, make small slits on it by using a tool Kowari, and obtain strands by bending it from side to side. The next step is to make Maru-higos by getting the strands go through holes on a steel plate. Sizes of the holes are from small to large, and the work is done from larger to smaller to obtain finely rounded higos. Rings that higos are supposed to come through are also made with bamboo. Like that for higos, trim the thickness by using Sendai, and put marks on where higos are supposed to come in. After putting the marks, heat the bamboo material, bend it in rectangular or circular shape, and get it cooled. Get the ends diagonally trimmed and closed up. The work to make the closed-up ends invisible is a chance for craftsmen to show the techniques. Get holes on where marked on the ring in rectangular or circular shape, and get higos go through the holes for assembling. In some cases, craftsmen get higos go through holes after a dozens of them are bent at once by touching them with a heated iron and cooled. Thanks to the higo bending work in different ways, a variety of fancy bamboo crafts become available.

將圓狀竹籤插入主體，用一種獨特的連接技法進行組合
駿河竹千筋細工的特色在於使用細圓竹籤進行製作。首先要製作竹籤。以尺測量尺寸再用鋸子切斷竹條，削皮後，用小刀標出必要的尺寸。接下來用「線台」測量厚度，再用雙刃小刀以縱向細割，然後用手左右折彎即可將竹條裂開。接著，將竹條穿過鐵板上的孔洞製作竹籤。孔洞從大到小，按粗拉、細拉、精拉順序依次拉伸便可以製作出精緻的細圓竹籤。用於穿竹籤的圓環也是竹子做成的。和製作竹籤一樣，用線台測量厚度後，在穿竹籤的地方標上記號。將標上記號的竹條加熱，折彎成圓狀或四角再冷卻。折彎後斜切再接合。能做到看不出接合痕跡也是技藝絕妙之處。在圓環和四角的框內標有記號之處鑽孔，接著穿過竹籤組合。把幾十根竹籤一起置於加熱後的棒狀工具上彎曲，冷卻後穿過框，依竹籤折彎的技巧可製作出各種不同設計的竹藝品。

して組み立てていきます。数十本単位でまとめた竹ひごを熱したコテに当てながら曲げ、冷ました後に、枠に通すこともあり、この竹ひごの曲げによって様々な意匠を凝らした竹細工が出来上がるのです。

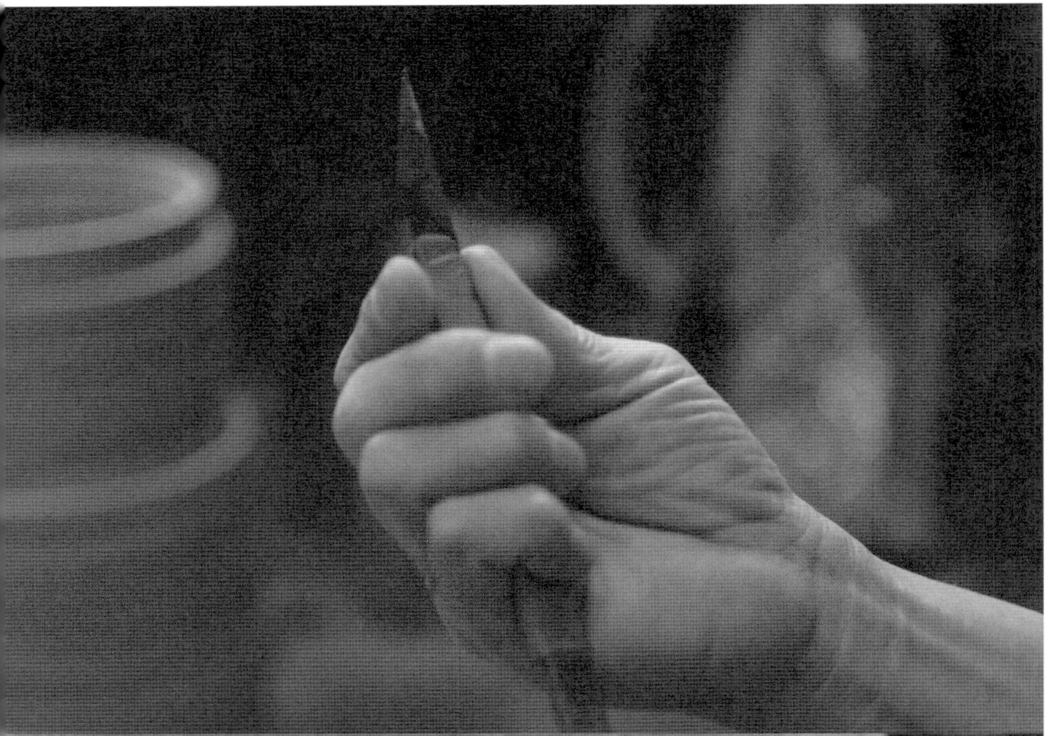
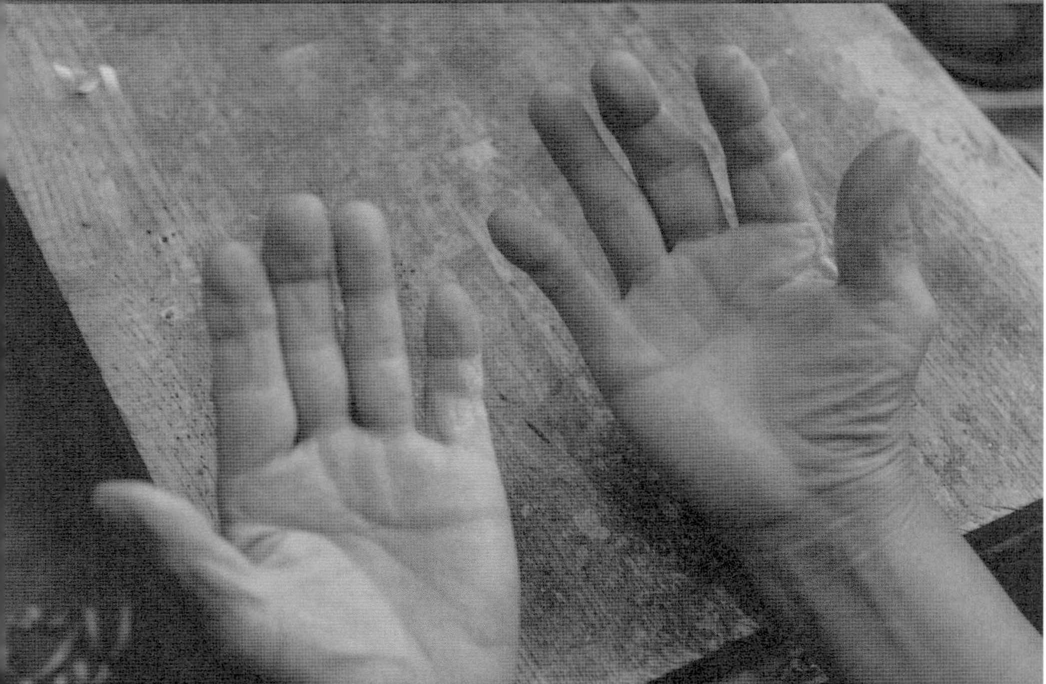

竹細工職人への道

Gateway to be a Bamboo Craftsman

成為竹藝工匠的路程

しなやかな強さを活かし、多彩な加工技法を駆使

竹を割く・削る・編むなどの技を用いて、竹製品をつくります。しなやかな強さを持つ竹は、曲げる・割るといった加工が容易なので、竹かごや茶筅（ちゃせん）を始め、釣り竿、弓、インテリア用品まで多種多様。日本の至るところで竹を採取できることから、竹工芸は昔から生活用品として身近な存在といえます。竹工芸は、竹選び、竹ごしらえから始まり、ざるは「編み」、茶筅は「割り」、弓は「削り」と製品によって技法が異なります。時には200以上もある工程を、ひとりの職人が手作業で仕上げていきます。全工程に匠の魂が宿るため、竹の性質を活かした耐久性や美しさがあるのは当たり前。そこに、年月とともに竹の艶、肌触りが増し、プラスティック製品などには真似できない質感が加わるのです。

Applying a variety of techniques, while benefitting from the robustness and flexibility of material
Bamboo crafts are produced with techniques such as splitting, shaving, and weaving. Works like bending and splitting can be easily done on bamboo because of the robustness and flexibility, and the products are offered in wide range such as from baskets, green tea muddlers, fishing rods, bows, and interior goods. Because bamboo can be harvested everywhere over the country, we have been familiar with bamboo crafts as our living ware since old times. Make of bamboo craft starts with selecting appropriate bamboo material and performing preparation work, and the process of make is different for different types of products, such that colanders are produced by weaving, tea muddlers are by splitting, and bows are by shaving. Sometimes more than 200 different processes are performed by only one craftsman by hand. Because craftsmen put their soul into all the processes, it is in the natural order of things that the products are offered with the robustness and beauty supported by the characteristics of bamboo itself. On top of that, the gloss and suppleness of touch of the surface of bamboo become evident across the ages, and rich texture that can never be obtained by plastics or any artificial products becomes appeared.

善用竹子強韌的特性，運用多種加工技法
以竹子為材，運用切、削、編等技巧，製作竹製品。因為竹子柔軟中又帶有強韌，易於折彎、切割等加工，從竹籠、茶筅，到釣竿、弓、室內用品等，種類繁多。由於日本到處都可以取得竹材，因此竹製品自古就廣泛用於日常生活中。竹藝從竹子的選材，準備作業開始，篩子用「編」的，茶筅用「割」的，弓用「削」的，製品不同其技法也各異。有時200道以上的製程會由同一個工匠以手工完成。由於全部製程裡都寄與了工匠的精神，所以運用竹子的特性所展現出的耐久性和美觀也是理所當然的。其中，竹材的色澤、觸感會與日俱增，而且還有塑膠產品等無法模擬的質感。

自分のデザインを開発。使う人の心を持って時代に挑む

ひとつの素材（竹）のみを使い、様々な技法を駆使して、何かを創作したいという人に向いています。また、竹選びで竹林に入った時に感じる青竹の清々しい香りも、楽しみのひとつ。加工する際も漂うため、竹の香りが好きな人にもぴったりです。竹工芸で大切なのは「使う人の心」になること。ひとつひとつの加工の技も重要ですが、使う人に気に入ってもらえなければ意味がありません。街を歩き回って、人・街並み・雰囲気を自分の肌で感じ取ることに苦心する職人もいるほど。加工がしやすい竹工芸は、時代の変化に柔軟に対応。新しい作品で、自分の時代を切り開く可能性を竹細工は秘めているのです。

Developing the own style, creating a new era with users' mindset
The work of making bamboo crafts is suited to those who are eager to create something new only with a single material (bamboo) but by applying a variety of techniques. One of the delights in this work is to enjoy fresh aroma of blue bamboos when you go into the forest to make your choice. As the aroma comes up also when you process the material, those who love the aroma of bamboo are also cut out for this work. One thing for the bamboo craftsmen to keep in mind is to understand the "users' mindset". Although needless to say each of the techniques is important, it is meaningless if the user become unsatisfied with the products. Some craftsmen thus take a walk in order to try to feel people, town, and the air by themselves. The bamboo crafts, associated with ease of work, flexibly adapt changes of the time, involving a great potential to create a new era with new ideas.

開發屬於自己的設計站在使用者的角度面對時代的挑戰
這項工藝只用一種素材（竹子），加上各種技法的靈活運用，適合有意創作開發的人。還有，進入竹林選擇竹材時能感受綠竹的清香，那也是樂趣之一。由於加工時也會散發出竹香，相當適合喜歡竹子香氣的人。在竹藝的世界裡，重要的是要懷著「使用者的心」。雖然每種加工技法都很重要，但若不能讓使用者滿意的話就沒有任何意義。有些工匠會特別花心思上街走走，自己親自去體會人群、街景、氛圍。竹藝的特色是加工容易，同時也能因應時代的變化。在竹藝的新作品中，隱藏著開闢自我時代的無限可能。

九州から関東に生産地が点在。技能士検定で、ワザを広げる

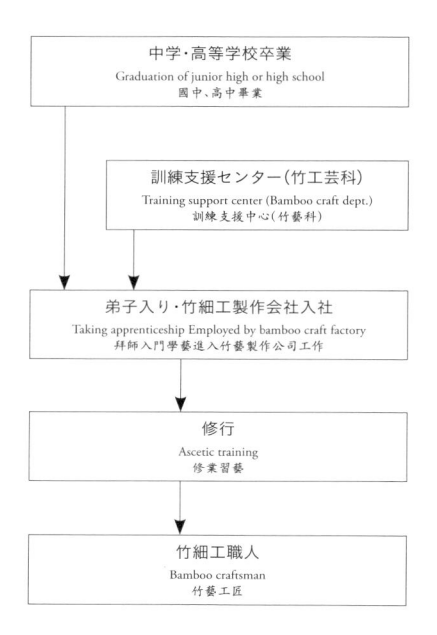

竹細工で有名な大分県に専門訓練校があり、竹工芸のワザを学ぶことができます。他にも、岡山県、大阪府、静岡県、東京都などの生産地で、弟子入りや竹細工製造会社への就職で道が開けます。現場修行で経験を積み、ワザを磨きましょう。

```
┌─────────────────────────────┐
│ 中学・高等学校卒業              │
│ Graduation of junior high or high school │
│ 國中、高中畢業                  │
└─────────────────────────────┘
              │
              ▼
       ┌─────────────────────────────┐
       │ 訓練支援センター（竹工芸科）      │
       │ Training support center (Bamboo craft dept.) │
       │ 訓練支援中心（竹藝科）           │
       └─────────────────────────────┘
              │
              ▼
┌─────────────────────────────────────┐
│ 弟子入り・竹細工製作会社入社              │
│ Taking apprenticeship  Employed by bamboo craft factory │
│ 拜師入門學藝進入竹藝製作公司工作          │
└─────────────────────────────────────┘
              │
              ▼
       ┌─────────────────────────┐
       │ 修行                     │
       │ Ascetic training         │
       │ 修業習藝                 │
       └─────────────────────────┘
              │
              ▼
       ┌─────────────────────────┐
       │ 竹細工職人               │
       │ Bamboo craftsman         │
       │ 竹藝工匠                 │
       └─────────────────────────┘
```

Areas of production widespread from Kyushu to Kanto, passing National Skill Test spreads world of techniques
There is a vocational school in Oita, well-known as a production area of bamboo crafts, where you can learn the techniques. Also in Okayama, Osaka, Shizuoka, Tokyo and some other area, you have opportunities to take apprenticeship or be employed at bamboo craft factories. Polish your techniques by getting experiences through ascetic training at a real production place.

九州到關東都有生產地。透過技能士檢定考試推廣技藝
以竹藝聞名的大分縣設有專門訓練學校，可以學習竹藝技術。其他在岡山縣、大阪府、靜岡縣、東京都等也有生產地，可以拜師入門或以進入竹藝製造公司工作的方式入行。直接親臨現場累積經驗來磨練技藝吧。

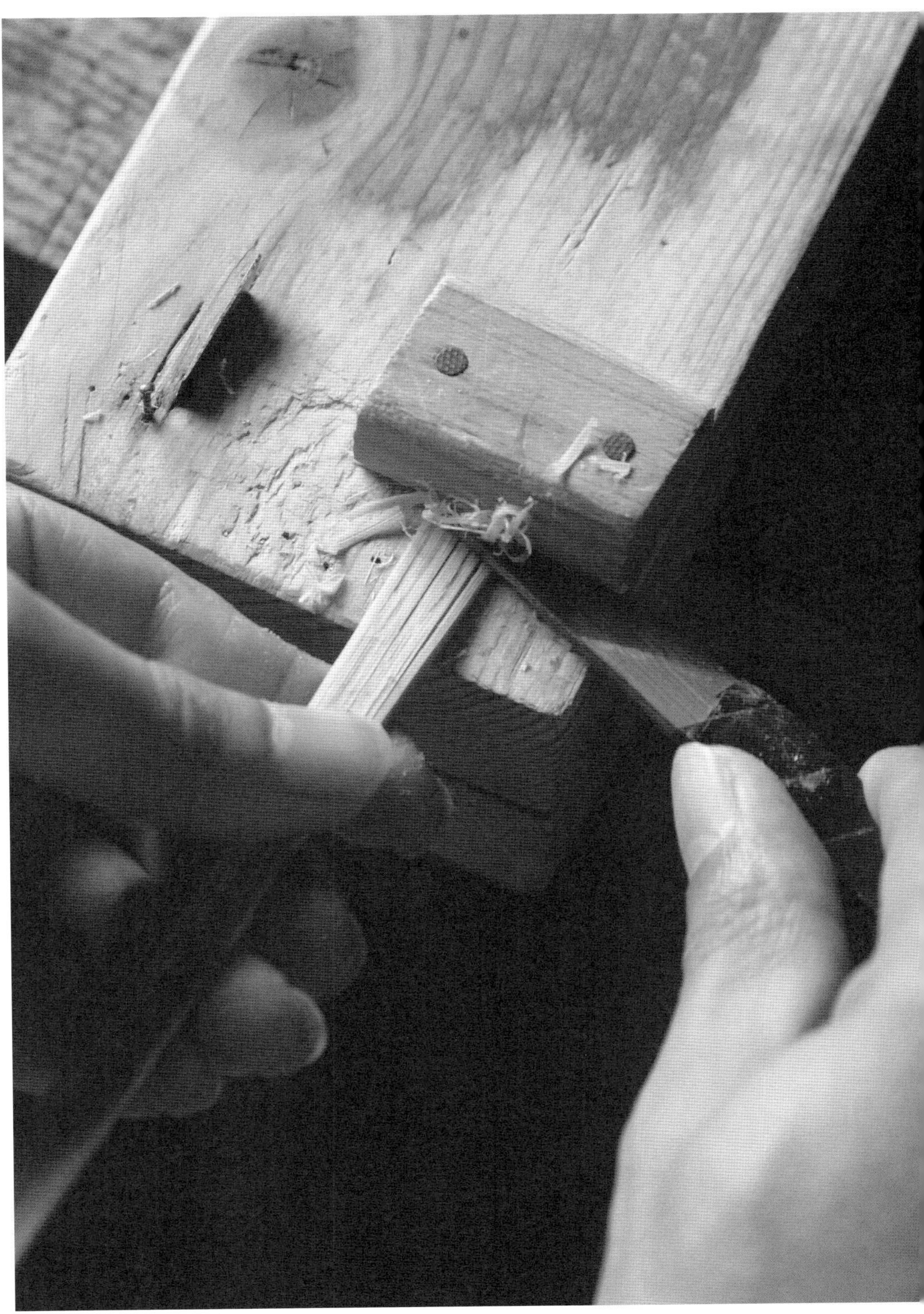

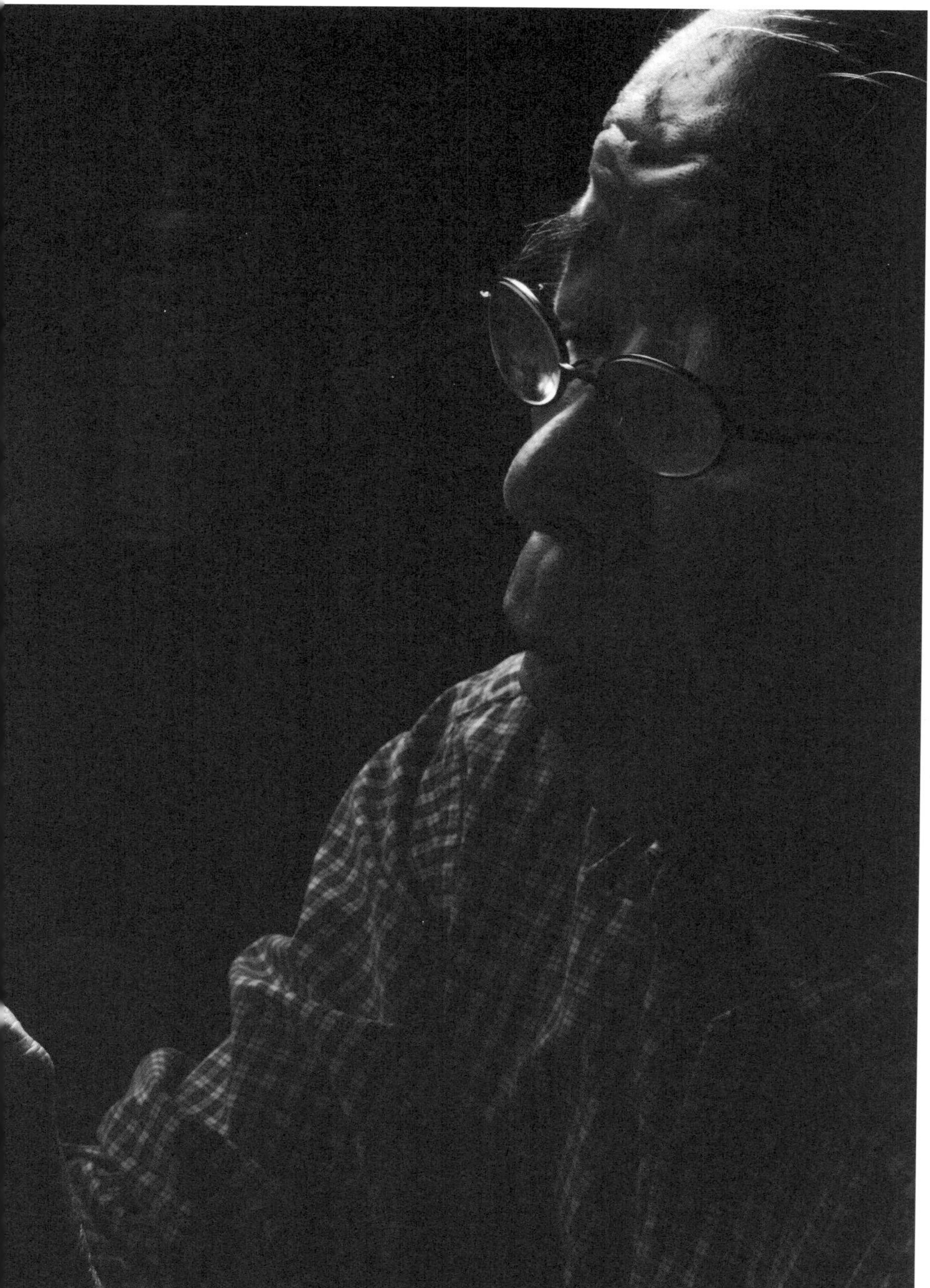

体験するなら　To Experience　體驗

静岡の伝統産業を家族で体験できる施設
体験工房駿府匠宿

静岡市駿河区丸子3240-1　電話／054-256-1521
営業時間／9:00〜17:00（各体験工房のお申込みは16:00まで）
※一部夏季期間の営業時間9:00〜18:00（各体験工房のお申込みは17:00まで）
休館日／年末年始　料金／おすすめ体験コース「竹千筋細工」虫籠1500円、花器1900円　他
HP／http://www.sunpurakuichi.co.jp/takumi/

A facility where the whole family can enjoy feeling Shizuoka's traditional crafts
Taiken Kobo Sunpu Takumishuku
3240-1, Maruko, Suruga-ku, Shizuoka City, Shizuoka
Telephone: 054-256-1521
Opening hours: 9:00 – 17:00
(Accepts application for experiencing factory until 16:00)
Opening hours in a specific period of summer: 9:00 – 18:00
(Accepts application for experiencing factory until 17:00)
Closed: Year-end and New Year
Fees: Recommended experiencing course "Bamboo Ware" insect cage for 1500JPY, Flower pot for 1900JPY, and others
Website: http://www.sunpurakuichi.co.jp/takumi/

可以全家一起體驗靜岡傳統產業的設施
體驗工房駿府匠宿
靜岡市駿河區丸子3240-1
電話／054-256-1521
營業時間／9:00〜17:00（各體驗工房的申請時間到16:00為止）
※夏季期間，部分設施的營業時間為9:00〜18:00
（各體驗工房的申請時間到17:00為止）
休館日／年終年初
費用／推薦體驗行程「竹千筋細工」蟲籠1500日元、花器1900日元等
HP／http://www.sunpurakuichi.co.jp/takumi/

学ぶなら　To Learn　學習

地域産業の「ものづくり手」を支援する制度
静岡市経済局商工部地域産業課　クラフトマンサポート事業

静岡市駿河区曲金三丁目1番10号　電話／054-281-2100
※研修生の募集要項など詳しい情報はHPなどでご確認ください。
HP／http://www.city.shizuoka.jp/deps/tiikisangyo/chiiki_koukeisya.html

A public system to support development of successors on local industries
Craftsman Support Program, Local Industries Dept., Commerce & Industry Department, Economic Affairs, Shizuoka City
3-1-10, Magarikane, Suruga-ku, Shizuoka City, Shizuoka
Telephone: 054-281-2100
For details such as application material for trainees, refer to the website.
Website: http://www.city.shizuoka.jp/deps/tiikisangyo/chiiki_koukeisya.html

支援地方產業「製作巧手」的制度
靜岡市經濟局商工部地方產業課 手工藝支援事業
靜岡市駿河區曲金三丁目1番10號
電話／054-281-2100
※欲知研修生徵才項目等詳情，請自行上網確認。
HP／http://www.city.shizuoka.jp/deps/tiikisangyo/chiiki_koukeisya.html

---

掲載の情報は2012年3月現在のものです。
詳しくは各施設のホームページなどでご確認ください。
The information printed here is current as of March 2012.
For more details please check on the website of each institution.
以上為2012年3月現在的刊載資訊。
詳情請上各單位的網站自行確認。

職人という生き方
駿河竹千筋細工

本書編集スタッフ

構成　　　　木下のぞみ
取材・文　　ニッポンのワザドットコム編集部
デザイン・装丁　棟田夏子（ブレインカフェ）
写真　　　　富野博則
校正　　　　荒木さおり（ブレインカフェ）
英訳　　　　古賀知憲

職人という生き方
駿河竹千筋細工

二〇一二年四月　第一刷発行

編者　　　　ニッポンのワザドットコム編集部
　　　　　　Ⓒ有限会社ブレインカフェ
発行者　　　木下のぞみ
発行所　　　有限会社ブレインカフェ
　　　　　　東京都中央区銀座四丁目十一―六
　　　　　　島倉ビル三階
　　　　　　電話　〇三―五一四八―五八一八（代表）
　　　　　　http://www.braincafe.net
印刷・製本　シナノ書籍印刷株式会社

定価はカバーに表示してあります。
造本には充分注意しておりますが、
万一乱丁・落丁がございましたらお取り替えいたします。
本書の無断複写（コピー）は著作権法上の例外を除き、
著作権の侵害になります。

Printed in Japan　ISBN 978-4-905416-03-6　C0072